The Grov

(Tune: "Shortnin' Bread")

Let's plant love and joy and patience;
Let's grow peace and kindness, too.

I'll dig a hole and you plant a seed.

We'll have fun when I help you!

 I'll give a hand. I'll give a smile.

I'll keep growing as God's child!

Let's watch rain fall on our garden;

Let's watch sunshine help seeds grow.

Let's pull weeds and we'll be patient;

We'll wait for good fruit to show!

I'll give a hand. I'll give a smile.

I'll keep growing as God's child!

Jesus Shows Love

Matthew 4:23-25; Luke 2:4-7,52; 24

**Find and circle the hearts in each picture.
Draw a heart, or put a heart sticker, next to Jesus in
each picture.**

1 Jesus is God's Son.
He was born in
Bethlehem.

2 Jesus grew up.
He helped people.
He told them about God's love.

3 Some people didn't like what Jesus said.
They killed Jesus. His friends were sad.
But Jesus came back to life!
Now His friends were happy!
Jesus loves us and He wants us to love each other.

Pony Pal Corral

Circle each person who is showing love.
Eight things are different between these pictures.
Draw an X on a number for each thing you find
different.

1 2 3 4 5 6 7 8

14

Our Bible says,
"[Jesus said,] 'Love each other as I have loved you.'" John 15:12

Jesus Tells About a Lost Sheep and a Coin

Luke 15:1-10

Jesus told two stories.

A Lost Sheep

There was a good, kind shepherd who had 100 🐑.
When he found one 🐑 was missing, the shepherd
didn't sleep.

Instead he started looking for the lost 🐑 so alone.
He searched until he found the 🐑 and brought it
safely home.

Just like the shepherd knows each 🐑 and cares for
them, it's true—
Jesus knows each one of us and cares for me and you.

A Lost Coin

A woman had ten silver 🪙; but when one wasn't there,
She cried, "Oh, no! One 🪙 is lost! I must search
everywhere!"

She searched until she found it. That silver 🪙 did shine!
She laughed and shouted to her friends, "I've found that
🪙 of mine!"

Jesus told the story of this woman's joy to say,
"When we become God's children, we give Him joy each
day."

Can you find the lost sheep and coin?
Color the B spaces BLUE.
Color the R spaces RED.
Color the G spaces GREEN.
Do not color the empty spaces.

God Gives Joy

Draw an X on the picture that doesn't belong in each row.

Our Bible says, "The Lord gives us joy." (See Psalm 126:3.)

God gives us people to love us.

God gives us food to eat.

God gives us ways to play.

God gives us animals to care for.

Session 3

Jesus Tells About the Birds and Flowers

Matthew 6:25-34

Jesus said, "God takes good care of the flowers.
He takes good care of the birds.
God loves YOU much more than flowers and birds.
He will take good care of you!"

Draw five red flowers in the grass.
Draw three blue flowers in the grass.
Color the birds. How many do you see?
How many children do you see?

God Cares for Us

Draw a circle around the things that might make you afraid or worried.
You can talk to God when you are afraid.
God will take care of you.

Our Bible says,
"My peace I give you. . . . Do not be afraid." John 14:27

Jesus Tells About a Patient Father Luke 15:11-24

A son asked his father for money, so he could leave home. His father gave him the money.
The son went to the big city. He spent ALL the money! He had to get a job feeding pigs.
The son was sorry for what he had done. He went home.

His father hugged him and forgave him. The father was very patient!

Help the son find his way back home.
Color the pigs on the path.

Patient Pals

Sarah is thirsty.

Draw

Miguel's dad is making dinner.

Draw

Peter needs the glue.

Draw

Our Bible says,
"Be patient with one another."
(See Ephesians 4:2.)

around the picture that shows Sarah being patient.

around the picture that shows Miguel being patient.

around the picture that shows Peter being patient.

Jesus Tells About a Kind Man
Luke 10:25-37

Use a 🖍️ to color the clothes of the men who were NOT KIND.

Use a 🖍️ to color the clothes of the man who WAS KIND.

Draw or stick a 🩹 on the hurt man.

Draw 🥔🥔 and 🌿 beside the road.

A man was walking on a rocky road.
Some men took his money and his clothes.
They hurt the man. The man needed help.
One man walked by and didn't help.
He was not kind.
Another man walked by and didn't help.
He was not kind either!
Then a man riding a donkey came by.
He stopped to help the hurt man.
He bandaged the man's cuts and took care of him.
This man was very kind!
Jesus said we should be like the kind man.

Caring Garden

Find the children who are wearing these shirts.
Copy the letters from the children's shirts onto the lines
under the matching shirts.
Tell how each child is
being kind.

Our Bible says,
"Be kind to each other."
1 Thessalonians 5:15

___ ___ ___ ___

31

Sticker Page